MAKING A ROUX

Also by Elizabeth Bewick

Comfort Me With Apples (Florin Press, 1987)
Heartsease (Peterloo Poets, 1991)

MAKING A ROUX

Elizabeth Bewick

PETERLOO POETS

First published in 2000
by Peterloo Poets
The Old Chapel, Sand Lane, Calstock, Cornwall PL18 9QX, U.K.

**A catalogue record for this book is available
from the British Library**

ISBN   1-871471-84-2

Printed in Great Britain by
Antony Rowe Ltd, Chippenham, Wilts.

ACKNOWLEDGEMENTS

Acknowledgements are due to the Editors of *Cross-Currents, Counter Currents, South* and *Other Poetry* in which some of these poems first appeared, also to Toni Savage of Leicester, who first printed some of them, and to Graham Williams of the Florin Press, who published my first book *Comfort Me With Apples* for permission to reprint 'The Seasons in Old Age', 'The Journey' and 'Visiting Day'.

'Come Back in Twelve Months' was short-listed in the 1991 Swanage Midsummer Festival of the Arts, and 'Redundant' in the Trimar Open Poetry Competition, Dorset, 1994. 'Angel of the North' was highly commended in the Portland Poetry Competition, 1998, and 'Climbing Beyond' won second prize in the Portland Open Poetry Competition, 1999.

'The Paradox of Spring' was produced in the Sonnet Pack by The Friends of the Cheltenham Festival of Literature, 1992, and 'Breath' appeared in *A Groat's Worth of Wit*, the selected entries to the Open University Sonnet Competition, 1998.

'Answer to Keats' "Ode to Autumn"' was published in the *Keats Bi-Centenary Anthology*, edited by Matthew Francis for the Winchester Festival of Literature, September 1995, and 'Riddle' in the *New Exeter Book of Riddles*, 1999.

INVESTMENT
SOUTH WEST ARTS

For:
Kay, Sylvia, and Lorraine
Geoffrey and Lyn
with love and thanks,
and, as always, for Richard.

Contents

Making a Roux

(for Maurice Rutherford, on reading his *Love is a Four-Letter World*)

No sooner off the page
than sounding in my head,
running along veins,
setting damaged heart
to dangerous old rhythms.

Lessons for age that I
must learn alone and late,
my mother walking in me
up the stairs, speaking
sometimes through me.

'The Light of the World'
book-mark in my bible
for my father's sake;
I remember the silences
for a different reason.

A nagging ache disturbs
my pillowed memories,
those things they valued
lost for all my caring,
when time made me a loser.

I never made a roux
before my mother died, her
cornflour sauce was good
enough for me, until I taught
myself the proper way.

The love that underlies
your telling lines
plucks a response from me,
so much I never learned:
you light the lamps again.

Mother's Day

Why
this day
more than any other
should I buy
anemones,
palatinate in memory?

Always
I remember
touching your hands,
tracing your life-span
for the first time
that evening.

Always
I remember
the horror of your dying,
and that I had not kissed you
when I left
that morning.

Returning –
beetroot and blood
mingling
on cellar stairs,
a half-made meal
your cold memorial.

So why
flowers today
more than any other?

The Hat Trick

(for Sean Street)

Not being prone to doing things by halves,
I fell from top to bottom of the stairs
in Maundy Thursday's still unfriendly dark,

and I'm the same age as my mother was
when she fell down our cellar steps and died.
That was Good Friday and I can't forget

the shock of coming home and finding her
not there, and never there again, though I
have kept her by me all these wanting years.

The shock of finding I was still alive
was quite another thing, and jolted me
out of the clutch of apathy and strain

and into recognition of my worth –
not half the woman that my mother was
yet still content enough to be myself.

Now, as myself, what can I do but this,
finish this poem? – start another one? –
a hat trick of disasters circumscribed.

My mother and my sister, dying first,
have left me in a strange way obstinate
determined not to waste the breath they gave;

to live accepting death's beneficence
is living more intensely than before:
I had to fall downstairs to find that out.

The Seasons in Old Age

(in memory of my father: James Bewick, 1884–1970)

SPRING
Spring is the hardest, all those thrusting shoots
and budding plants, the greenness of their youth
making a mockery of my own gnarled roots,
and youth's impatient seeking after truth,
its stark division into black and white,
strict honesty, no kindly shades of grey
to blur the outlines, dim the sun's clear light
and blunt the knife edge of a fine Spring day.

The lovers in the park, their arms entwined,
their bodies moving silently in tune,
if they could read my thoughts, would it unwind
their skein of joy, and will it all too soon
be tangled on the loom of man and wife,
relentless ravelling of daily life?

SUMMER
The greenness of the Spring gives way to glow
of Summer colour, rampant once again,
reminding me of flowers I used to grow
on disused pitheaps, smoothed into a plain
by calloused hands of workmen, making space
for growth of beauty out of levelled stone;
a garden in that barren smoke-grimed place,
brilliant with colour from the seed I'd sown.

But now the risen sap is poison's dart,
its deadly menace to my hands and feet
pinning me helpless here with alien heart,
wordless and worthless in the Summer heat,
an exile in this sunny southern clime,
as out of place as I am out of time.

AUTUMN
Autumn is kinder than the Summer's heat,
its colours red and amber without green;
the orchard smell of apples strangely sweet,
and purple quinces I had never seen
in northern gardens, where my life was spent
in growing richly variegated flowers,
passing the time in friendly argument
with fellow gardeners in the evening hours.

Now that my hands are useless tools of pain
others must dig the soil for worms to turn,
while I sit idly by and wait for rain
to cool the itch and act as balm for burn;
all those rich shades of russet at my feet,
leaves turning brown, then black, for compost peat.

WINTER
Winter at last and new contentment lies
on hands serene beside the burnt-out coals –
the fire that my forefathers worked to prise
from earth's dead heart through narrow blackened holes –
the workings of my mind washed clear by truth,
old snapshots sepia in the dying flames,
I talk again with comrades of my youth
and walk in company of vanished names.

And she who was the breath of life to me
keeps closest to me in the moving throng,
her smile of welcome, still a willing fee,
sustains my vision though the waiting's long:
if she, like God, can all my sins forgive
then death will be a better way to live.

The Road Back

(For Betty Wise)

A black armband road, mourning a cut
as clean and savage as a butcher
might have made, swinging his cleaver
across defenceless countryside,
the Nidd, the Ure, the Swale, valleys
bridged, the old ways almost hidden.

On up the Dales, a well-loved track
climbing steadily between the fells,
their green sides surely velvet
to the touch; patterns of stone walls
criss-crossing the fields, stone barns
squaring up to the north-east wind.

Streams swollen into tranquillity
by melted snow, yet every now and then
waterfalls leaping from crag to crag,
their energy reminding me of childhood,
of jumping over the rocks and falling,
my father confident I wouldn't cry.

Arriving in Cumbria, where he
bought me my first K sandals, took me
walking in the hills, I think of him
all day on this Remembrance Sunday,
his image clear against the backcloth
of northern landscape that he loved.

I polish his medals, lay them out,
think of him returning from the war
they said would end all wars, ill and
almost certainly disillusioned.
I wonder – did he find it worth it,
a first headship and a second daughter?

The Small Dark Man

Warm in my central heating
draught-proofed and double-glazed,
with windows steaming
when I run a bath, I feel
remembered chill of bathrooms
when I was a child: the frost-etched
patterns on the glass, the cold
striking through dark brown lino
where I sat, numb fingers
turning the pages of my father's books.

Grim company, a goblin
lived down behind the bowl,
harmless if I kept still, but
waiting to pounce on me
if I was not downstairs,
safe in the lighted hall,
before the noise of flushing
died away. He scared me then
but nothing stopped me reading,
cold on the lino on the bathroom floor.

Reading in bed – my mother
taking off my spectacles
and putting out the light –
I woke to feel the moon
striking my face, strange shadows
slanting on the edge of sleep,
creatures grotesque and menacing
poised for attack, a nightly army
out of brightly papered walls,
the patterns I had chosen for myself.

My sister, eight years older,
caught me hiding her copy
of *The Small Dark Man*
face inwards on the shelf.
I thought she'd never understand
until I found she knew, about
the goblin living in our loo,
endured worse things than creatures
crawling from the walls,
confronted her own terrors of the night.

The Gap Between

Always one step ahead,
an envied giant stride,
that eight-year gap between
your wisdom and my need.

Nothing could ever be
too hard or strange for me
that you had done before
and smoothed my way the more.

So death is now a step
that one day I shall take,
a giant catch-up leap
I need not fear to make.

Released by Stone

To sit on sun-warmed stone and gaze on trees,
a distant mass of green, to look between
them to a stretch of sea, a dark blue line
streak thin but bordered by a brooding haze
from which the mountains rise surprisingly.

To wait and let words come, if come they will
to comfort grief or calm post-mortem fears,
or let my anger rush out in a rage,
retrieving feelings pushed onto a shelf
without the need to hate God or myself.

This is the freedom that I needed most:
released by harmony of sea and stone
from bondage of my walled-in thoughts and words,
I can accept a sense of history
and settle into timelessness alone.

House Clearance

How short a time it takes to clear a life:
a day spent emptying cupboards and I flaunt
two pairs of sandals for my lovely sister,
a poor exchange by any sort of count.

We never were the same size anyway
and looked at things from different points of view,
yet I sort her belongings with perception
and read their record of her life anew.

My understanding sharpened by my grief
I see her artistry in all she used,
presumptuous to think that I can match it
that passionate attention to the truth.

Now empty rooms are cold and walls are bare,
stripped of the colour that her paintings gave
but resonant of total dedication,
integrity preserved into the grave.

●

Late Exhibition

Your pictures sing along my walls
I watch their colours glow and spread,
the light from painted sunshine falls
around my dazed and dazzled head
but you stay obstinately dead.

I see the pathway, feel the grass
a living green beneath my feet,
I watch the evening shadows pass
and find the morning sunlight sweet
but you and I no longer meet.

I climb the mountain, walk the road
and know again the way ahead,
you always took the heavy load
I only followed where you led
and you stay resolutely dead.

Circles

Resounding circles of coincidence
go ringing round our heads after a death,
our lives enriched outside experience
by what our friends told while they still had breath
and what they tell us now; their words spread light
in language healing as a sacrament,
their vision widening our blinkered sight
beyond the reach of human measurement.

We wear our memories, the polished sheen
of jewels at our throats and in our hearts
reminding of commitment to the past,
proclaiming what its influence can mean;
others observe this radiance, which starts
fresh circles of coincidence that last.

Inheritance

I lay on sand before I lay on silk,
not shifting sand: hard, firmly ridged and moist,
speckled with grains from feather-beds of rock
wind-driven from the fast-eroding coast.
A line of dogged pitmen gave me birth
whose way of life was rugged as the shore,
they hacked at stubborn seams below the earth
and hewed a living under ocean floor.

Their women walked full-breasted in the streets,
reared children to mind well a father's word
and hid their work-worn hands of twisted bone.
Aroused from sleep I lie in silken sheets
remembering the accents long unheard,
uneasy with a choice they can't have known.

Continuity

(for Kay Cotton)

Warmed by a real coal fire with flames for dreams
and music bringing memories to life,
I touch the Portland stone from which light streams,
whole for the first time since my sister died.
Here, where her things are fittingly at home
and gentleness unfolds their polished gleam,
there is a quietness so long unknown
I had forgotten how such peace could seem.

I throw brown sugar on the dying fire
to watch the blue flames shoot into the air,
I get undressed beside the still warm pyre
and dream of childhood as I brush my hair;
it was my sister's brush and now is mine,
a promised continuity of time.

Angel of the North

Brooding, the landscape waits, the hill-top site
which might have been a megalithic mound,
later a coal-mine, closed and grassed above.
The men who dug for coal beneath the ground
hewed a hard living, cut off from the light,
each man dependent on the one in front
part of a moving line of Davy lamps.

Uneasy black-faced ghosts, they wander now
across terrain they cannot recognise
and call a marra's greeting into space.
As ninety thousand motorists each day
hurtling their way up north, raring to cross
the bridge above the Tyne, go heedless past
the new road settles into history.

Long over-shadowed from across the Tyne
once called 'a dirty lane to Newcastle',
Gateshead now bursts with noisy civic pride
and plans a giant engineering feat
twice as spectacular as any ever known,
dwarfing achievements of past centuries
outdoing Penshaw, rivalling Tyne bridge.

Vast angel balancing in space and time
will challenge concepts of immensity,
standing four double-decker buses tall
with wing-span wider than a jumbo jet,
an access door on giant shoulder-blade:
a statue that will dominate the scene
straddling the north, angel with ribs of steel.

In Memoriam Frank Spears, 1906–1991

New-planted saplings, their light wooden stakes
more like the crosses in a Flanders field,
now line the route I used to drive to you
and, taking it again this afternoon
to pay you one last visit in farewell,
I thought their starkness seemed appropriate.

Yet Easter flowers bloomed inside the church
and we remembered you with joyful songs;
I saw you with a sudden clarity
wearing your skull cap, specs pushed off your nose,
eyes bright with mischief – *I'm a Jew*, you said
and then I knew for sure you were not dead.

The Paradox of Spring

Bereavement is incongruous in spring,
the grey of loneliness bears winter's mark
and grieving is more fitting in the dark,
when wild things sleep and birds no longer sing;
long dragging hours of winter almost match
the dreariness of spirit deep within,
and heaviness of heart seems less a sin
than an infection anyone could catch.

But this exquisite burgeoning of bloom,
the lush abundance of a new-sprung green
and rising sap in everything that grows,
evoke bewildered anger when one knows
no comfort, other than what should have been
encompassed by the heart's now empty room.

The Journey

Just off to see your friend?
So lucky you live here
and near enough to see her when you like.
Nice place there, isn't it?
Such lovely grounds they have,
and everyone so well looked after too.

You taking that for her —
made it yourself, did you?
She always liked your cooking best of all.
A nasty cold you've got —
oh, just catarrh, you think?
Well this damp weather doesn't help, you know.

A bit depressed, are you?
Come now, we can't have that,
there's always something to look forward to.
Must dash now, back to work,
can't stand and talk all day,
I'm sure you'll feel much better in the Spring.

I pick my blinkered way
along the narrow path
between the cottage and the river bed.
My feet move to the car
with automatic steps,
my mind already reaching out to them.

Each was a person once,
with family, children, job,
responsible for other people's lives;
each now obsessed by age,
with stockings wrinkled down
and loosely-fitting knickers all displayed.

Will this be a good day,
one of the better ones,
when she can whistle, laugh and try to talk?
Or one of the reverse,
no smile to calm my fears,
no recognition there of anything?

My face arranged with care
I walk into the heat,
the stench of urine meets me at the door.
And how are you today?
I'm fine, dear, how are you?
I scan the row of chairs to find the face I love.

Visiting Day

A crowded room, stale smell, those patient souls
on rows of chairs, waiting to die, or sleep,
holding their crumpled cards with anxious looks,
no way to show their gratitude but weep.

Each locked within herself, no way to speak
the hopes and fears that wake the mind to thought,
yet wordless comfort for each other's hell
and childless pleasure for a moment caught.

They chatter without sense, and cluster round
the curtained window, watch the streaming rain,
wave to each other's friends, and settle down
in two straight rows of apathy again.

And we, how can we bear to leave them there,
knowing that out of sense is out of mind?
A jester babbles wildly of green fields,
and in that room a life is left behind.

The Pit

(for Graham Lea-Cox)

What is this force that pulls you down
away from my encircling care?
  Two grasping hands with wrists of steel
  that drag me deep into a pit,
  where blown-out skulls and wind-picked bones
  are waiting till I join them there.

What is this gall that makes you thirst
and drink the mineral water dry?
  A metal roof inside my mouth,
  lined with unfashionable fur
  that tastes of mould and rotting flesh
  and dries my tongue to bitterness.

What is this nightmare in your head
that turns your eyes away from me?
  An endless showing of old stills,
  remorselessly recurring themes,
  my private gargoyles, loosed from hell,
  a silent scream from open mouths.

What is this blackness in your soul,
dark fear of death that shuts out light?
  Not death but life is what I fear,
  the endless, grinding, going on,
  relentless day succeeding day,
  the years strung out ahead of me.

Images Before Sleep

Caught in a brush-stroke on a page of light
the sinuous movements of the belly dance
become a dual piece of artistry.

Is pride in an achievement such a sin?
Do bouts of self-disgust show greater worth? –
these life-enhancing patches irritate!

Long nights are troubled and the winter days,
though short, are piercing with relentless cold –
what hope is there of warmth without my love?

The storm clouds gathered in the east are full
and dark with nuclear malevolence
that could unleash all hell upon the earth.

Preoccupation with one's own concerns
is self-indulgence in a world at war
where unremitting prayer would better serve.

Pain wraps me in a comfortless embrace.

What?

What have I left to show
for more than seventy years
of doing and being? –
a small skill with words,
a capacity for listening?
It has to be enough,
I have to find content
within myself, not look
for help from husband,
support from absent lover.

Children never born
give me no grandchildren,
no family likeness
links me to the future,
my stake in the past
is buried with my sister.
Only my will to cling to
as evidence of present tense,
I trust my feelings, wrestle
with words to clothe them.

Age of itself has little
worth, experience is no
magic charm, nor wisdom
something given with the years,
and what I am I owe as much
to grace as circumstance.
My certainties less sure
as prejudices fade,
the heart accepting change
is searching still for truth.

Breath

Flat comfortable shoes of common sense
worn all my life, and still I drag my feet
up easy slopes, those mountains of deceit
against which breath now offers no defence.

Where poets meet, steep open stairs are blamed
for my slow climb. I stop and count the heads
seen through the spaces in between the treads:
my fellow critics curiously framed.

Breath comes more freely once the magic works,
we share our dreams in words upon the page,
communicating bursts of grief or rage
and drawing strength from criticism's quirks.

Wordsworth and Coleridge must have wrangled so
to balance needs of rhyme with rhythm's flow!

Herb Pot-Pourri

Roses bloom early in a heat-wave Spring,
already I make yellow pot-pourri
from full-blown 'Peace', each petal tinged with pink.
I have to use left-over lavender,
the hedge is only growing cuckoo-spit
and it's too soon for that compulsive haze
that passing strangers brush against and nip,
sniffing their fingers as they walk away.

I pick fresh rosemary, whose scented spikes
remind me to pay tribute to the past,
to bathe with it removes all trace of age
but I'm not certain that's a risk I'll take:
we first get on with life, then shape our verse
out of the pattern that the years have made.

Self-Questioning

Is it the sudden falling that you fear
like falling into sleep but twice as sheer,
or is it walking in the dark alone
along an unmarked route to the unknown,
is it uncertainty that chills your breath
and leaves you trembling at the thought of death?

Is it the colours that you hate to leave,
half-finished patterns you had hoped to weave
into a tapestry with strips of rag
stored carefully inside your sewing-bag,
can you not leave the finishing to one
who knows exactly how you want it done?

Behind the Door

(for Matthew Francis)

Maybe it will stay outside,
not push its face
into the space
behind your mind,
maybe it will keep away
not leave its mark
beyond the dark
or mirk of day –

go and close the door.

When night is bright
with hurting light
and day comes late
with crippled gait,
even if night's
just half as bright
and hurting day
is on its way –

go and close the door.

Through hours of dark
now bright with pain,
grey shape again
grows whitely stark,
as edge of dream
is shot with fear,
that evil leer
is almost seen –

go and close the door.

At least then
it will stay outside,
while light of night
and dark of day
together hurtle
on their way,
to leave no space
for you to hide –

go and close the door.

That shuffling, gliding,
pointed shoe,
just glimpsed beneath
the door's thin crack,
will have no chance
to weave and tack
across the floor
and into view –

go and close the door.

The Peep-Show

(for Mr J. McGrand)

Steel symmetry of piping overhead
throws out of focus patterns on blurred sight,
their strangeness in the silence of the night
accentuates our consciousness of dread.

An early roll-call brings new confidence,
a reassuring bustle of concern
pervades the ward. I lie in back-slit gown
one eye dilating in a circle dance.

The waiting hours behind my pirate patch
drag out their space and give me leave to think,
gauze mask across my face, a pin-hole blink
gives access to the needle's thread of thought.

As hush of theatre envelops me,
caught neck and heel on narrow metal bed,
square sapphire suns are flashing overhead
and ermine moth wings settle on my eye.

My lids ooze tears, I try my new-found sight
and, taking courage, walk into the light.

Hallucinations

(for Mr P.C. Gartell)

The lights come on in butcher's shops
where sheets of undressed tripe have lain,
once scraped they can be trimmed like chops
and stewed to tenderness again.

Tarantulas in thousands crawl
below the surface of my skin,
their hairy legs in rise and fall
have penetrated deep within.

Computer clocks that whirr and bleep
still punctuate exploding time,
though ageing bodies lie and weep,
denied a part in pantomime.

The nightmare shifts, the curtains fall
and only half my mind believes –
in spite of dancing at the ball –
behind those curtains there are thieves.

The ceiling drops in squares of light,
pinks, yellows, blues, go swimming round,
lift and descend in crazy flight
to leave their burden on the ground.

The crosses on the path outside
reflect each colour in its turn,
accentuate the thin divide
between the day and death's dark urn.

The scar below St. Catherine's Hill
is covered by a mercy cloud,
but diggers in the distance still
shriek their destructive skill aloud.

The dawn, a full-flushed apricot,
bursts through the new-washed eastern gate,
irradiates the ward's deep rot
and sets the record almost straight.

Redundant

(for Geoffrey Armstead)

It's strange to have no face. They
should be the faceless ones, who
scurry past my still-drawn blinds,
heads down against the rain,
dark-suited, executive hands
clutching locked brief-cases
close and secret to their sides.

It's strange to have no name. They
should be the nameless ones, who
queue outside my office door,
shut only for a time
to give each privacy to talk,
ask questions, seek advice,
need me – but I am not there.

It's strange to have no eyes. They
should be the sightless ones, who
sit with one drink in the pub,
lonely when others leave –
the lunch break over – their gaze
fixed, blank with pain, wrenching
focus from my need to theirs.

'Come Back in Twelve Months'

(for Mr R.M. Rainsbury)

Allotted span of threescore years and ten
and then one more to celebrate the rest,
to wait and speculate on whether fate
has something up her sleeve, new game to play,
after the fine excess of seventy springs.

A year of celebration and of hope
yet, looking back, I see it as a year
taut with expectancy and fraught with fear;
the passing days were a kaleidoscope
as childhood dreams and visions rocked the dark.

Some women wear bright colours to deceive
themselves and others facing bitter truth;
wearing my purple with a jaunty air,
leaving a trail of perfume in my wake,
I flaunt my vaunted courage in the street.

Tomorrow brings new knowledge where I stand
in freedom with my thoughts and my desires,
wearing the pattern of my vibrant year
for all to see the colours that appeared
and glowed more strongly through long months of doubt.

Riddle

Black my beginning:
shape of a siren
talons for fingers.

Round and full after:
still warm to the touch
safe cupped in my hands.

Full circle my whole:
oil on a puddle
or gleaming shot silk,
myriad colours
imprisoned in glass,
globe floating on air.

(Answer: Witch-Ball.)

Workshop

We write about cane chairs and memories,
fathers just home from work, or hospital;
I see the continuity of history
in the minutiae of recollection,
but I am shaken suddenly to life
by others' raw acceptance of a death.

We cogitate about the use of metaphor,
ill-chosen adjectives and nouns mis-used,
ask for more space between the paragraphs
as though the thing we're looking at were prose,
while high above the smoke-screen of our talk
a poem sings its individual song.

Cliff's Edge

(for Brian Hinton)

I who cannot readily
see pictures in my mind,
only words, can see it still:
that house at the cliff's edge
all passages and stairs,
its unexpected rooms
piled on haphazard floors
to reach the sky, the sea
breathing everlastingly
a window's breadth from your bed.

Bondsman in that place, straining
at the ropes that hold you,
caught in a sort of freedom
that fevers you and frets,
you brood over your books,
play out old melodies,
watch as the tide comes in
to lap the hard cliff's edge:
the sea's a chilly mistress
never quite inside your bed.

Witch-Ball

I walk into the inside of my own head,
discover a network of pathways,
broad roads and narrow ginnels,
all of them leading in different directions
with no regular pattern,
no apparent order or cohesion
(and I live by order – or think I do)
no light or colour,
the eerie thinness of a wood in winter.

I choose one at random
hurry down an easy slope,
then pull up short
half-way up a steep hill –
gradients no easier
inside the head
than in the world outside.

Frustrated, I carve my own way,
crossing tracks cleared by my ancestors,
feeling the pull of ancient ley-lines.
I creep around in smaller and smaller circles
getting closer to the space in the centre,
where I can just see the small nut
that my brain has recently become.

Reaching it through a tangle of overhanging branches,
trampling the undergrowth
and pushing aside a scatter of twigs,
I make a sudden resolution:
lifting its cold, dead weight,
feeling rough edges hurting my hand,
I muster all the strength I thought I'd lost,
break it in two and dash the pieces on the ground.

Out of the blackness inside
a bubble is airily released,
floating, as if blown
from a child's clay pipe –
a witch-ball of colours,
red, blue, purple,
shot through with silver,
my private globe of revelation.

Sleeping Upstairs

(for Sylvia Miles)

I have never slept upstairs when here before –
treads taking too much breath – but now I see, front
the long wall of grey-white Portland stone, too high
to look over from below, back to the sea
and Kay's shed, private and shut against the wind,
her place in which to think and write her poems.

I spy over the wall at prison chimneys,
the wind bites as I walk up the new-made road
with its smoothed-out hairpin bends. I stop for breath
and to photograph the pattern of the sea
in my head, the length of the causeway beyond,
the strange construction of this almost island.

Following the path back towards the quarry
I find the ferns and flowers that Sylvia picks.
She left a vase of them in my upstairs room
where I can sleep hearing loved voices below –
I wake at 6 a.m. to hear a child laugh
and turn to sleep again, knowing all is well.

Greek Images

It seemed I had no skill
with which to stitch
my tapestries, spirit
crushed, long nights
strangely suspended in time,
grey weight of fear.

Now, night is shot with
needlepoints of light,
a mesh of gold scratched
on the bottle-green
that is the surface of
the sea on which I sail.

Pomegranates, such as I
have only ever eaten
with a pin, are ready now
for Hallowe'en in miniature,
their yellow lanterns
ghostly, wicked, in the trees.

A hedge of morning glory,
purple in the afternoon,
keeps from the sun's rays
lemons still small and green;
leaves from a banana tree
fan me to sleep at night.

Something I had thought
quite wizened stirs to life,
new growth is painful
but genesis of pleasure
as my spirit turns,
lifts to the sun again.

Climbing Beyond

(for Kay Cotton)

It took me four years to climb, hand over hand
up narrow stairs, leaving the darkness behind
to look through wide windows open to the sea
and the long ridge of pebbles, their wet sharp tang
mingling with the smell of dust from quarried stone,
stung nostrils breathing in salt and headiness.

I'd always wanted to see over the wall,
not just the blue-veined hills in distant outline
but things close to: the quarry's machinery
from which strange clanking noises echoed all day,
stark grey-white chimneys of the prison building
with its unexpected church, but always locked.

For so long my back was turned against the wind:
facing it, I walk away from the prison
towards the sea. No longer a barrier
the causeway becomes only a narrowing;
leaving familiars behind, I walk through
sure now of the strength to face what lies beyond.

Abbotsbury Pottery

The sea is in it, surf-topped blues and greens,
a scattering of smudges in sand brown,
blotches of white from pebbles thrown by waves
onto the shore, size-sorted, smoothly ground.
They say a Dorset man, caught in a storm
washed up on Chesil ridge, would find his way
by feeling for the pebbles at his feet,
their size a guide until the daylight came.

Holding this curving bowl I trace the sea
explore the roughness of the shingle beach,
its pebbles warm against my finger-tips,
the finest almost gone beyond my reach.
I stretch towards them, peer across the bay,
feeling the roundness of the potter's clay.

Meditation on a Brown Bowl and a Wind Farm

(for Marie Coleman)

Clay shaped to fullness, sensuously rounded,
out of the darkness shadows subtly changing,
light from within soon shedding its abundance
through slow discernment.

Hands cup its meaning, hold the message captive,
draw meditation from its smooth perfection,
eyes gaze in wonder, see from mind's high window
work of a craftsman.

Arms of the windmills flailing on the hilltop
carving the sky in segments of direction,
tossed by the wind's chance, thrown into confusion
slowing to silence.

Out from the bowl's depths curling shape of movement
rising in spirals, leaping as to music,
lifting the heart to whirl in frenzied patterns –
warmth from its dancing.

Amber Is Its Own Colour

(for Lyn Moir)

Amber is its own colour, pale
or dark, translucent or opaque,
oily to the touch, redolent
of pine from primeval forests,
ointment or good soap. Fossilised
insects trapped within its depths are
specks of darkness. Warmth flows from it
and myth wraps it in mystery.

Tears that Meleager's sisters
shed after his death hardened
to amber. I found mine in Greece,
tracked down through narrow alleyways
to small shops, dimly lit, back-lined
with glass. Flowing in waterfalls
of sound, soft hammer dulcimers
made music of antiquity.

Amber washed up on Baltic shores
clings to the seaweed's underside,
collectors rake it in their nets.
My amber cross is Latvian
bought at a craftsman's market stall;
his hands were steady when he carved
its shape, mine shake a little as
I touch the sheen of holy oil.

Too Many Levels

I didn't have my ears pierced
till I was seventy-five, and
now my friends are nagging me
to paint my toe-nails.
Why should I listen to them?
I don't like painted nails, and
anyway I've got a hammer toe
that nearly kept me out of the Navy.

She doesn't ever get bored,
my neighbour, and there she sits
stark naked at the piano
for hours on end, always practising.
Why can't I be like her,
not bother about what people think? –
living has too many levels
and I've always felt the cold.

I'm getting there gradually,
polished my shoes on the table
last week, my mother must have turned
in her grave, except that we had her
cremated – it was what she wanted.
I could have been on the films
but I played too hard to get
and priced myself out of the market.

The world of computer speak
attracts and repels me by turns.
I too could live like that,
send letters by fax and e-mail,
walk around with a mobile 'phone,
have a chipset motherboard.
I could make love on the Internet
or would that be too theoretical?

No Clothes and No Toes

No clothes and no toes,
a battered doll, laid
carefully against my cushions.
I introduced her to my owl
and covered both of them
with an old shawl so that
they lay incongruously close,
blonde curls to velvet ears.
Once she was covered
she was just a doll again,
not nakedly reminding me
of what I had been told
of a torn childhood,
of isolation and rejection.

The child, thumb in her mouth
hand pulling at her hair,
looked at me fearfully
and back at her sleeping doll,
picked up my owl, and –
with an oddly adult awareness
of our role as conspirators –
kissed him quickly on the beak.
Then for the first time
her eyes became alive,
she climbed on my knee,
pulled at my chain
and threw short strangling arms
around my neck.

Blue Moon

Happiness wakes me to a child's delight
in knobbly parcels stacked beside my bed,
the opening of eighty years of stored
anticipation, tinsel coronet,
gold wrapping, canary-yellow flowers,
purple vase. Miniature roundabout –
set fair for speed – twirls at a touch,
its jewelled arms catching the rising sun.

Wild peals of bells make clamour in my head
and crashing chords of words ring round the room;
the moon slides down the sky and out of sight
empty of its custodian, who swung
blue and beak-nosed, wearing gold epaulettes,
saluting from the lamp-post all night long.
The day is mine I thought would never come –
I hug my blue balloon and laugh at age.

To Wildly Go ...

(for Mathew and Creina Francis)

Already an octogenarian
I am seized with an absurd desire
to live outrageously –
more wildly than before
if that can be sustained.

I remind myself of a friend
who fancies his chance
as a womaniser,
but is too much addicted
to being loved by his wife.

I could flout the conventions
if I'd not done so already,
break rules and hearts,
flaunt late sexuality
loudly and with panache.

I could declaim my verses
from tree-tops too high
for climbing,
set my blue-moon balloon
swinging in crazy circles;

lean out in my birthday suit
in the new-made light of dawn,
finding my inspiration
in the guessed-at goings on
behind neighbours' net curtains.

I could live on smoked salmon
flown in from Skye, develop
a liking for oysters,
take to drinking bloody Marys
in spite of not liking vodka.

None of this is outrageous
enough; at twenty
I dried my hair in the garden
wearing a flamboyant kimono,
waving to passers-by.

In a Washington heat-wave
I wore my designer pyjamas
to all the best parties;
at eighty I wear them
to answer the door, nothing more.

Spider in My Navel

(a poem on a painting by Amanda Welch)

Suddenly I want to break out
to shock and surprise,
so I paint myself in colour –
as colour almost:
bright yellow skin,
nipples – one blue, one green –
perched on my breasts like birds
singing aloud but out of tune.

A small spider sleeping in my navel
rearranges its legs,
the yellow of my stomach heaves
as I try to pull it away.
Is it the one that fell out of my pillow
when I made my bed this morning,
and where in my private darkness
did it spend the night?

My hands, two different shades of green,
shudder away in disgust,
shrink from spider contact
and gravitate towards my pubic hair
encased in a net,
not a conventional hair-net
more like the cover on my goldfish pond,
designed to keep the gold in its place.

I shy away from the significance
of the blood,
red on my legs
and red below my breasts,
a blood-red background
to this portrait
of myself –
there are some things I will not paint.

House of Girls

(for Richard)

Beth is the shy one
still not sure of her profession –
I only keep her on
because she pleases you,
most demanding of my customers.

She welcomes you at the door
fusses over you,
makes you feel important,
brings you brandy and coffee
to alleviate the stresses
of the day, the long drive here.

Lizzie runs your bath
softened with perfumed oils,
her skilful fingers
massage the tension from your body
till you sink deep in the waters.

Isabeau wakes you
running her fingers
through your hair, arousing
with wasp-tongued kisses
the liquid passion on your lips,
soft in the unaccustomed morning.

But it is I, Elisavetta,
who am the Madam;
when you tire of my girls
I dismiss them to their cubicles
with a practised flick of my wrist.

It is I who wait on you
in the heat of the day,
until we neither know nor care
if it be noon or night,
day-break or sun-set
behind the close-drawn curtains.

I minister to your needs,
bringing more brandy and coffee,
smoked-salmon sandwiches,
and *Fanny by Gaslight*
which we read to each other in turn.

I take off my negligee
and the spray of orchids you gave me,
my grandparents' photographs
in the gold locket I always wear
nestling incongruously
between my naked breasts.

Only I have a key to this room –
the girls are not allowed –
but we both know
that when another morning comes
it is Beth who must send you back.

Aegean Island

(for Bonaros Petros)

From Galatas I look across the strait
see Poros set in lapis on the shore,
cloud mountains moving in and out of space
framing a picture I could never draw.

Sailing around the island we pass rocks
covered with mountain joy – wild marjoram;
we buy some later in a mainland shop,
rub it between our hands and take it home.

Hoping for fish in Little Biski Bay
the boatman throws a thin thread line to sea;
bouzouki music scares the fish away –
he laughs, reels in his line and talks to me.

Returning late to bougainvillea's flame –
a royal welcoming – lilies off-white
to palest apple green, their trumpets blown,
give heady perfume for just one more night.

Postcard from the Aegean

Strong smell of olive oil and fish,
taverna two feet from the boats,
changing light on lapis water,
sun setting behind the island
stringing pink pearls across the sea.

Skies stretching out the mystery
of space, houses climbing uphill,
wide squares and narrow alleyways,
bougainvillea flaming from
walls blue and white with postcard paint.

Tracks twisting over the mountains
incised by the indigent goats,
roads winding on and up, to find
Epidavros, sleeping lions
and the stone theatre of time.

Stones speaking the ancient myths,
epics alive in glimpsed faces,
always a sense of belonging
both to the present and the past,
Greek drama breaking through the skin.

Seen in the Alresford Gallery

(for Brian Knowler)

Tin peacock and stone hen beside wrought iron balustrade
pecking the ground as I have seen them do in Greece, harsh sun
singeing the bare hillside. Here on a patio in shade

set in the soft contours of the Itchen Valley, they preen
glossy unruffled feathers, toss strangely unmoving heads,
while golden fishes swim the waters of a blood-red sea;

lifting blunt noses from the turbulence they gasp for air,
each round gold eye fixed on the one in front and rigid fins
dodging a blue-veined peacock in a circular despair.

Mist in the valley shifts and rolls around the room, soft grey
settles across the landscape where the long low chalk hills brood
hiding folded secrets till the ways of the Maze be plain;

steel-blue, the painted sky is overlaid with yellow corn
sheaves whose frilled edges ruffle up the clouds, till with a shout
primaeval myths explode, clouds burst in violence of storm:

colour invades the earth, landscape in abstract is reborn.

The Challenge

(a poem on a painting by Jennifer Rosser)

Straightforward or surreal,
you take it either way:
a baby elephant, big-eared
with half-grown pointed trunk
and strangely spindly legs,
running in terror or mischief
from authority. The figure
in the background, a stern
and disapproving Edwardian
aunt or governess in hugely
decorated hat, changes at a
turn of head or flicker of
myopic eye into a wolf, savage
but still young, and nervous
of the part he's meant to play.

Strong dark splodges of a bitter
green, three shades of blue
from bright to sinister,
a lurid pink, patches of cinnamon,
the splattered black of stage;
an area behind the wings seen
through a gap between two poplars,
standing like twin black besoms
ready for use after the performance.
A predatory shark, deep petrol blue,
looms menacing above a cuddly
sheep-dog's head, dark green;
presumably it's made short shrift
of paws and tail – the corps de ballet
had better be nifty on their pins!

Peloponnisos

Parking to the shadow
cast by two cypress trees,
tall in their national pride,
a back-cloth of olives
set in dead straight lines
across the hillside,
jagged mountains behind;
the sea stretched out
a precipitous drop below,
shot silk but silvered.

Combing the beach to find
a clutch of sea-shells,
rough-edged and strange
but fitting exactly
one inside another; then
a perfect sea-anemone –
old-fashioned shaving brush,
bristles with military precision
growing out of stone
smooth and hard, a pumice.

Finding our way to Corinth,
the Temple of Apollo – seven
Doric columns bright in the
hot sun – headless statues
all around; a vision of St. Paul
preaching to the Corinthians.
Praying in a nunnery,
voluminous black skirts
kilted around our trousers
in orthodox discipline.

Plucking white mulberries
with no red stain of guilt,
lemons, limes and oranges
falling at our feet as we walk.
Hostility a tremor in the air,
the war in Kosova a sadness
never far beneath our thoughts,
our prayers a rosary
heavy with supplication,
a komboloi for peace.

Komboloi – a string of beads used as a plaything or a kind of rosary. The Greek
komboloi is usually made of amber and has anything from about six to sixteen beads
loosely strung.

Answer to Keats' 'Ode to Autumn'

I never quite believe you wrote it here
for Winchester's a place to be in Spring,
returning wonder of the new-made year
would make the most lack-lustre poet sing.
The city lies encircled by its trees,
their leafy freshness lifts the heart to God,
though ancient and Druidic trunks would seem
more fitted to acclaim a pagan birth
than winter's prisoned kingship to redeem;
the thin green, you called chilly, clothes the earth
to cherish summer underneath the sod.

For me ripe Autumn's mellow fruitfulness
is over-rated in your famous lines:
we've more dank days than sunny cloudlessness,
mist gathers in great lumps to top the Downs,
clings to the hair and penetrates the nose,
lies damply on our ungloved hands and seeps
through to the very marrow of old bones.
The trees shed moisture in the wind that blows
and fallen leaves are gathered in sad heaps,
their once-bright colours trampled as they lie
unheeded in the path of passers-by.

And yet the muted tincture and soft tones
of Autumn's palette strangely serve to bless
the solid structure of monastic stones,
enhancing their encrusted timelessness.
You would find Winchester still much the same,
door knockers you admired for sober mien
still sport a kingly lion or horned ram
that housewives polish to a quiet sheen,
side streets around the Close are still sedate,
old maids play cards or some new-fangled game
but none disturbs the silence after eight.

Response to 'The Red-Funnelled Boat'

(for Peter Armstrong)

Your words are rough
scraping the powdered surface,
a layer of otherness
that lies unbonded
on my well-creamed skin.

I want to rub my face in them,
to feel the brisk loofah
of honest gutturals,
to hear the broadened vowels
of a Durham man.

I need to ride the bus
through Spennymoor
from Four to Five-Lane-Ends,
a pitman's whippet
nuzzling against my leg.

To shop in Sunderland,
looking for Harris tweed –
a coat for northern winters –
waiting at snow-bound corners
for a connecting bus.

I can't go back –
privation shaped my lineage,
but I've lived too long
away from clemming coldness
and the knife-edge winds.

Lemonodassos

I never thought I'd see real lemon trees
dropping their casual fruit upon the ground
inches beyond my furtive fingers' reach,
would smell their pungent sharpness all around
steep-rising groves, or climb the stony path
to learn their terrain in the pauses meant
for healing, as I fought for breath
inhaling air rich with reviving scent.

Climbing the last few feet with bursting lungs
I came upon a view to stop the heart:
not just ripe lemons – limes and oranges
stretching below me to the turquoise sea,
their very colours smelling wild and tart,
the lemon juice they brought me fiercely sweet.

Full Moon over Neorion Bay

You came to your fulfilment
tonight but majesty is lonely,
your gaze, lambent and full,
has wistfulness in it.
I imagine you, aloof
in the night sky, enviously eyeing
clusters of golden lights
shaken into signs and symbols
up and down the hillside.
Reflections send flat-bladed swords
into the water as though, along
the coast, warriors stand ready
to spring to your defence.

A passing boat, garish
with too much light,
slips between twin beacons
at the harbour mouth, leaving
a swathe of velvet
smooth on the wrinkled sea.
You, who have seen so much
of voyaging, are unperturbed.

Beneath your gaze, men sailed
across the seas, leaving
small votive offerings
on gold and silver hooks
as bribes to plead safe passage.
You waited with Penelope
for Ulysses' return, staunched
her long years of weeping
and answered her fond prayers.
Tonight I pour libations
of my own, to pay you homage
and to make a special plea
that I may come again.

Farandole

(for Joan Sherratt)

Falling under an old spell as we go north
enchantment spills over to the present tense:
heat gathers closely, high priestess sits beneath
a cool white ceiling striped with blackened beams,
her face serene, around her neck a scarab
on a faceted gold chain, its glinting eyes
always alert to guard against intrusion,
while a unicorn gentles its mistress' sleep.

Two metal herons, tesselated markings
on black wings, lift darting heads sudden and swift
to kill; blue Abyssinian cats stretch necks
glossy and smooth, proud to be aristocrats;
a pair of moggies, podgy as black bears, squat
on fat haunches, folded paws tipped with white ruffs;
a clutch of painted birds peck wood in rhythm
to a child's command, and painted horse still rocks.

Cloisonné butterflies spread wings of flame to
hover above our heads, gold jester in his
tasselled cap sits on a down-pipe jauntily,
sundial set on chimney pot measures talk;
pottery chessmen serve delicious food, we
eat at low tables mopping wooden trenchers,
drink mead from striped brown cups, wine from old goblets
poured by wooden waiters, skeletal and tall.

We move through layers of history by walls
made of York stone: brown bears are lumbering down
Stoneygate, jugglers catch hoops, a busker plays
silver flute; time unobtrusively rethreads
my web of fantasy to sounding patterns,
oboes and flutes, clarinets and saxophones,
trumpets and drums, explode in a farandole.

The light of a long northern evening leads
home across the moors to where all fantasy
began, all images converge and sleeping, lie.

Valentine Dragonfly

(for Richard)

Who wants to read poems about arthritic hands,
the pain of angina, the frustration of being deaf
or not being able to see well enough to drive?

Yet these are my preoccupations in February, when
the weather is dank and depressing, and a lift to
the supermarket has to be regarded as an outing.

I would write poems about my dreams, but I don't
seem to dream any more – perhaps it's the effect
of new drugs – and a nightmare makes poor reading.

I never found the golden road to Samarkand, Arabia
is as far away as it was in my childhood, while
Popocatepetl has become merely a word in a book.

But, today, your Valentine dragonfly shot through
my letter-box, emerald wings a-shimmer and long
slender body straight as a silver spear in flight.

So now I cherish my dreams again, polish my pen
and write my verses bright on the ring of time:
the wheel still spins, years leave me unafraid.